Say More by Doing Less

30 Ways to
Grow Your Brand
While Saving
Time and Money

BELINDA CUTHBERT

CONTENTS

AUTHOR'S ACKNOWLEDGMENTS

Hindsight is an amazing phenomenon.
It is in hindsight that I realize that every accomplishment in my life
has only happened because I've been supported by amazing people.
It's with this in mind that I'd like to thank those who have stood
behind me over the past few months, not only while writing the
book, but also while making the decision to leave the corporate
world to pursue a new career.

To my friends at the Standard Bank Group. There are too many of
you to thank by name. Thank you to those who invested your time
in me while I was at the Group. So many of you helped to shape
me both as an individual and a professional.
To "The Comms Team" in particular - Tanya, Tony, Naseema and
Abiye. I consider it a privilege to have spent my working hours
with colleagues who felt like family. The decision to leave was a
difficult one, made easier only by your support.

To my editor, Tanya Early. Your feedback is always spot on. You
read every document as if it has the potential to be a best seller and
you always give it your best, whether it's a newsletter or a novel. I
appreciate that about you.

To my coach, mentor and friend, Estelle Pretorius. You've walked
a long journey with me. You were there when my desire to start my
own business was just a spark and you've walked the entire road
with me to this point of actuality. Thank you for your wisdom,
encouragement and friendship.

To my family. You smiled, nodded and gave me your blessing
when I told you what I planned to do. (Even though I know you
were apprehensive on the inside.) It's your unconditional support

that helped me make the tough decision and big changes.

I have the privilege to be able to thank three sets of parents. My Mom and Dad Horak, Mom and Dad Cuthbert and Mom and Dad Lawther. You are continuously sowing hope into my future which has made it easier to envision a more fulfilling life. Each of you has done so much for me and there is no way that I can acknowledge it all. Your role has been greater than you can imagine.

To my husband Geoff. You didn't even flinch when I told you I wanted to start my own business. No more salary. No more benefits. No more bonus. You just said - "no problem". What would I do without you? Thank you for seeing that I wanted to become something more and for backing me all the way.
I love you.

To my children Keegan, Samantha and Jason. You're the reason I'm pursuing something new. How could anyone look at three amazing creations like you and not want to be better each day? I want you to realize that everyone can pursue a career that can make a difference. For me, I want to see people reach their potential. For you it will be something else. It is there for the taking. Go for it.

No acknowledgement would be complete without thanking our Heavenly Father. It is only through Him that we can take leaps of faith without fear and move into promises of a future that's bigger than we can imagine. There is no honor in doing anything unless we do so to honor Him.

It is my hope that you will take the knowledge in my book, apply it well and - when you begin to benefit - that you will use your success to make a difference.

Belinda

FOREWORD BY RAYMOND AARON, NEW YORK TIMES BEST SELLING AUTHOR

I spend a great deal of my time travelling all over the world, coaching and teaching business owners on the topic of branding your business. I've worked with all business types and sizes - from the solopreneur through to those fortunate enough to work with a team by their side.

I've shared the speakers stage with global icons such as Dr Nido Qubein, Sir Richard Branson and Dr John Gray. I have battled the challenges of owning my business and have come out triumphant on the side of success.

Why am I telling you this? Not to blow my own trumpet, but to tell you that I've been around the block. I have felt the pain of being a struggling business owner and I've also felt the exhilaration of seeing my plans come to fruition. Mostly I've seen a common truth in every single business person I've interacted with - big and small. The truth is that your business cannot and will not succeed if you do not put huge amounts of effort behind branding yourself as an expert in your field.

Growing your brand usually takes a lot of time. It involves both online and offline marketing and you need a lot of message content to keep these efforts going.

Until recently, the only options available to a small business was to outsource the content production at huge costs or to do it themselves at a huge expense to your time. Time that you should be spending on running your business.

Say More by Doing Less provides a third alternative. A combination of a "done-for-you" and "do-it-yourself" content solution that won't leave a hole in your pocket or a burden on your diary.

Belinda is an expert in the field of Corporate Communication. Shortly before writing this book, she decided to dedicate her time to helping entrepreneurs and small businesses find solutions to their own communication needs.

This is the first of her business advisory resources. What Belinda has to share will offer you a surprisingly easy solution to connect with your customers and draw in new prospects.

Small businesses need to hear about this time saving, cost effective kick start to branding activities. It is my humble opinion that small business owners should grab hold of this lifeline with both hands. Get your name out there, brand yourself as an expert and watch your business skyrocket.

Maybe one day, I'll be sharing the stage with you as you share your own story of growth, success and business achievement.

Raymond Aaron

Raymond Aaron is a speaker, author and adventurer. He has committed his life to teaching people how to **dramatically change** *their lives for the better. Today, Raymond is helping people achieve greater wealth, branding, recognition, confidence, respect and authority. Raymond teaches his clients how to become respected authorities and experts in their fields.*

Raymond has shared his vision and wisdom on radio and television programs for over 20 years. He is the author of 8 best-selling books, including **Branding Small Business For Dummies, Double Your**

Income Doing What You Love and the co-author of *New York Times* best-seller **Chicken Soup for the Parent's Soul and author of the Canadian best-seller, Chicken Soup for the Canadian Soul.** *He is also an avid adventurer having completed one of the world's toughest races, Polar Race (a 350 mile foot race to the Magnetic North Pole). This trek to the North Pole has inspired his newest title,* **How You Can Get Rich Without Getting Cold.**

INTRODUCTION

How this book came about

I left the corporate world six months prior to writing this book. After thirteen years of being a Corporate Communication Professional, I wanted to pursue a freelance career in writing. I specifically wanted to start my own writing practice and focus on providing business content to small businesses and entrepreneurs.

It wasn't long before I realized the extent to which a busy life in a corporate environment had protected me from the realities that small businesses face in a troubled economic climate. Through my interactions with my new clients I observed that, for every business that could afford a freelance writer, there were dozens that couldn't.

I found myself increasingly drawn to the stories of businesses who were straining to keep head above water. I stood at a crossroad. I could choose to keep only those clients who could afford to hire a writer or I needed to develop a more cost effective model of providing content. I chose the latter.

I began to explore a type of writing that my coach and friend had introduced me to before I left the corporate world. This form of writing is called "Private Label Rights" or "PLR".

PLR is both a time saving and cost effective way to buying content for business messages. A PLR writer prepares content to the same standards that they would for any freelance project. The difference comes in with the selling. Rather than selling the completed article only once for the full writing fee, it is sold to a number of different customers at a fraction of the cost. The intention is that each buyer will customize the content until it is unique to their business.

Buyers who choose to use PLR are therefore able to afford great business content and also have the accompanying rights to make any changes they feel necessary. Using PLR as business content is common practice in many countries but I had never seen it used in South Africa, my home.

As I spent more time exploring the PLR practices, it became clear that this could be the solution for many businesses who need to market themselves on a tight budget.

The solution is not exclusively designed for cash strapped businesses. While some use it to save money on their content budget, others simply use it as a time-saving solution for their marketing needs. Mostly, it's used for both of these reasons.

So, with that, I added PLR to my portfolio. The more I pursued the topic, the more excited I became about its possibilities and I wanted to share the solution with small businesses. Hence this book.

Say More by Doing Less is a direct observation of what I have discovered and experienced over the past six months as both a writer and small business owner entering the world of online business.

I have gained the utmost respect for entrepreneurs and small businesses - people who have stepped out of their comfort zones to build a future for themselves and their families.

My goal is that my book will spark renewed hope in business owners and help them believe that it is indeed possible to build a business that will attract more sales and success without spending excessive amounts of time and money.

What will we cover in this book?

This book is written specifically with entrepreneurs and small business owners in mind. More specifically, for those who are new to the world of online marketing techniques.

In Chapter 1, we'll focus on content. What is content, why do you need it, and how much do you need to be considered relevant in online marketing?

I'll then introduce you to Private Label Rights content. I'll explain what PLR writing is, what to look for in a PLR provider and what your rights are as a PLR buyer.

We'll then explore how you can take a PLR article and re-purpose it into at least 30 different ways to grow your brand. Although the majority of these 30 methods are online marketing techniques, we'll also look at other more traditional offline marketing ideas.

We'll end off by looking at some practical marketing combinations using the 30 methods discussed in this book.

In addition to the information between these two covers, you are also entitled to bonus material which you can claim from our website www.thecommunicationshop.com under the tab "Say More by Doing Less". The resource report will contain more information about some of the resources mentioned in this book as well as resources that I have found useful in my business.

PART 1
CONTENT

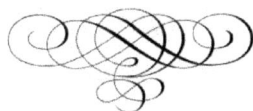

1 MESSAGE CONTENT

What do we mean by "content"?

In very simple terms, "content" is the body of any message that you place in the public space. Your content could be writing (text), images, video, or audio content.

Your content could be "online" or "offline". The term "online" refers to information placed on any internet based platform, while "offline" refers to the use of the more traditional, non-internet based media.

A business that wants to grow its brand must learn to use a combination of text, images, video and sound and to use these in both online and offline applications.

Every potential customer has a preference in terms of how they want to receive information. Some prefer watching a message in video format while others enjoy reading text based articles. Some enjoy finding information by browsing websites while others prefer buying magazines. As business owners, we need to learn to use a variety of media to cover our customer preferences.

Regardless of which content format you use or whether you focus your efforts on online or offline, one thing is sure - you need a consistent flow of content to stay top of mind in the public eye and one step ahead of your competitors.

In the last half of this book, we will show you how to take a PLR message and adapt it for a variety of online and offline uses.

How can you use content to grow your brand?

People have been using helpful content to brand themselves as experts since the days when cave art was still popular. The earliest example was found around 4200 B.C. A cave drawing was used to share information which scientists loosely interpreted as "Six ways a spear can save you from a wild boar." I bet you that guy was popular.

Of course, it didn't end there. History is filled with examples of businesses that distributed valuable information with the intention of indirectly increasing sales. Here are a few examples:

- In 1985 John Deere launched its customer magazine "The Furrow". The magazine has remained popular with a loyal readership and today is distributed to 40 countries in 12 languages.

- In 1900, the tire manufacturer Michelin introduced "The Michelin Guides" to help European drivers maintain their cars as well as find decent lodging when travelling. The original intention was to promote travel and with it increase the sale of tires. The guide is now distributed across continents and is more popular now than a century ago.

- In 1904, Jell-O distributed a recipe book, free of charge, which helped it achieve more than $1million in product sales by 1906.

- In 1922, Sears launched a store radio station with the intention of keeping farmers informed during the depression crisis. The content was supplied by Sears Roebuck Agricultural Foundation. (Content Marketing Institute)[i]

The list of examples goes on and on. It wasn't until the late 1990's that the theory behind branding through useful content was acknowledged as a formal marketing discipline. In the early 2000's Penton Custom Media of Ohio, coined the term "content marketing".

I personally love the description that the *Content Marketing*

Institute offers for content marketing:

> "Basically, content marketing is the art of communicating with your customers and prospects without selling. It is non-interruption marketing. Instead of pitching your products or services, you are delivering information that makes your buyer more intelligent. The essence of this content strategy is the belief that if we, as businesses, deliver consistent, ongoing valuable information to buyers, they ultimately reward us with their business and loyalty." (Content Marketing Institute)[ii]

In the next section we'll discuss how content marketing can help you grow your brand.

SAY MORE BY DOING LESS

2 BUILD YOUR BRAND USING INFORMATION

How can information sharing help build your brand?

One could write an entire book just on the principles of good Content Marketing, but since it's not the core focus of my book, we're only going to take a brief look at a few of them. There are many great resources on the topic for those who want to explore this further.

Here are the principles that I've chosen to highlight for now. Content Marketing should be done in a way that can help:

- establish yourself as a thought leader and expert
- attract people without forcing sales
- build loyalty by introducing the human element into your business messages
- attract customers from all corners of the globe
- provide easily accessible information
- grow your list of followers
- get a better view of your audience
- improve your Google ranking

Let's look at each individually.

Establish yourself as a thought leader and expert
The information you provide reflects your level of expertise and

knowledge of your field. This means that providing a continuous flow of high quality content will serve as an endorsement of your ability and will ultimately help you stand out in a competitive environment. When the content you provide helps address questions and concerns in your target market, then you will also be considered someone who adds value to the lives of your customers.

When a customer needs to choose between two similar product offerings, yours and a competitor's, they will more likely believe that you are the wiser choice because of your perceived level of expertise. Be sure to back up this perception with the high quality products and services that customers expect from an expert.

Attract people without forcing sales

The purpose of content marketing is not to make a sale. It is to provide solutions to questions and then build a trust relationship so that customers are more open to sales proposals when the time comes.

Build loyalty by introducing the human element into your business messages

When writing content, mention your employees' names, and refer to them and occurrences at work. Use real photos of your people and real life success stories where possible. Be authentic in your delivery as this helps foster a personal connection, open relationship and loyalty.

Attract customers from all corners of the globe

With roughly three billion internet users, we have the potential to attract customers from every corner of the globe almost effortlessly. If people on the other side of the world like your information it increases the potential of expanding your business footprint in future.

Provide easily accessible information

Online connectivity makes it easy for useful information to be passed from your customer to their contacts. Social media has become the new word of mouth and messages spread literally within seconds. The more interesting and useful the information, the more likely it is that it will be forwarded, liked, pinned or posted. And that's what every business wants. Your reputation is strengthened when conversations are started around your content.

Grow your list of followers

Online business uses two terms not often used in the offline world. These are "leads" and "lists". A "lead" is a person who is possibly interested in your product and the "list" is the database of people who have given you permission to add them to your marketing email list.

Content marketing improves your leads (attracts potential customers) and encourages people to join your list (marketing database). People on your list will be more open to receiving promotional offers from you since they have already received value in the form of useful information. This may make them more susceptible to making a purchase of some kind. In short - the larger your list, the more potential for sales at a later stage.

Get a better view of your audience

The two-way nature of the internet gives you an opportunity to gain a better understanding of your audience. Ask customers for information in return for a free information product to thank them for their time. The information can help you adapt existing products or create new ones to provide a better solution to the public.

Improve your Google ranking

Google is by far the most popular search engine in the world. So it stands to reason that you should do whatever it takes to make sure that Google pulls up your business information when someone does a search in your niche. The higher you rank on the front page of a Google search, the better your chances of the user clicking on your site.

How do we do that? By making Google happy.

In simple terms, Google favors pages that they consider to hold the best information for their internet visitors. Google continuously crawls the internet, scanning content and indexing all pages. When someone does a search, Google pulls all related pages from their index and ranks them according to relevance. As a business owner you will want Google to consider you as one of the most relevant pages for that search.

Google uses over 200 factors to compare your site to the other 60 trillion pages on the internet to determine your degree of relevance. Although nobody, except the Google engineers, knows exactly what the 200 factors are, it's public knowledge that:

- Google prefers pages that are updated regularly and contain fresh, up to date information. Static pages definitely don't rank as highly as pages that are updated regularly. The more often you update your website and social media accounts, the more favorable you will be during a search.

- Google also loves big sites, that is sites with a number of subpages. The more content you produce, the bigger your site will be and the higher its relevance in the eyes of Google.

- Google ranks your presence as being more relevant if there are a lot of back links to your site. A back link is when the link to your site is referred to in someone else's online messages. If people enjoy (or even hate) your content they will share your link with their friends, mention it on their blog, send out emails, social bookmark it, tweet or Facebook it. The more your links are featured in other people's profiles, the more Google will index you as being relevant. It stands to reason that you will have more opportunities to be back linked you when you share information more regularly.

- Long tail keywords give you an edge. One of the best

reasons to produce content is the opportunity to be found during an internet search because of the words used in your URL long tail.

A long tail is the name that appears in the address of each individual page on your site. For example, if my main URL is www.thecommunicationshop.com and I create a page for my CustomWrite™ content then the long tail (or additional key words) for this particular page could be www.thecommunicationshop.com/customwrite/plr.

Google will search through each of these page names to find relevant information for its users. A user searching for "PLR" may not know about my online store, but may still find it in a search because my long tail contains the keyword "PLR".

This becomes especially effective if you use a blog contains its own long tail keywords. Remember to use powerful keywords in your long tails. (Google)[iii]

Your readers will come back for more

Good, fresh content is the key to maintaining a consistent flow of traffic to your site. People don't go back to browse stale sites that never change. Don't miss out on potential return visits. Make sure you regularly update the information on all your internet locations. It doesn't mean you have to blog every day. You could combine your efforts by alternating your updates on your site and your social media profiles. Don't have people coming to your site 3 or 4 times without seeing any new content. You will lose them.

To summarize, content marketing is a great way to grow your brand. Businesses that provide the public with valuable information will be rewarded with more loyalty than businesses that don't do the same. The challenge is producing a continuous flow of high quality content.

SAY MORE BY DOING LESS

3 AN EXPERT REPUTATION

What type of information can you distribute to grow your brand?

Every business has a wealth of information that is valuable to the public and, if offered in a professional way, this information will make the business appear to be more of an expert in the field than the competitor down the road that does not reach out to the market.

So what type information should you distribute?

Information should complement your business. You don't want to give away trade secrets that will make your list independent of you, but you do want to offer relevant information that will have them coming to you for more.

The best way to illustrate this is to look at some practical examples.

1. A Success Coach

Based on your skills and experience in coaching people to success, you will have heaps of general information that you could provide to your list. Imagine the sense of loyalty you could create in readership if you share information such as:

- Five tips for New Year's Resolutions that won't leave you feeling like a failure.
- Eating habits of the successful.

11

- The link between attitude and success.
- Kick-start your week with proper planning.
- Sleeping habits of highly successful people.

I've only provided five examples but the list of topics is endless. You could even break these examples down further into subtopics, for example:

Sleeping habits for:

- ...successful business owners.
- ...problem solving.
- ...renewed energy.
- ...busy moms.
- ...students.

Being more specific with the choice of topic means that you can begin to target messages to very precise segments of your target market.

The more people lock onto your information, the more you will be considered an expert in your field and you will attract a greater following. A loyal following is the key to word of mouth referrals.

2. A Freelance Accountant

As an accountant you don't need to show your audience how to balance their own books or submit their own company tax returns since this part of how you make your money. However, but you could provide the following type of value add information:

- Five surprising tax breaks you should consider.
- Top ten apps for recording your monthly expenses.
- Why increasing staff benefits is a financial advantage.
- An easy-to-use checklist to prepare you for tax season.
- Teaching your children the value of investing.
- Seven reasons to get professional help for personal tax returns.

There are countless topics that can add value to the client without making them independent of your services. Imagine providing that type of information under your business brand -

showing that you are not only available during tax season, but that you are an expert who knows how to add value at any stage of a relationship with a customer. And what will this do to referral rates when someone asks your current customers to recommend a good accountant?

Remember, you are looking to grow your brand - your reputation. And by doing so, grow a loyal list of followers who will remember you when they need to hire a professional.

3. A Restaurant Owner

Let's use the example of an upscale restaurant. You want people to choose you rather than the restaurant next door when it's time to make their next dinner reservation.

Your messages could include article titles such as:

- How to choose the perfect wine to compliment your meal.
- Eat smart when dining out.
- How to enjoy a meal out while on a diet.
- Five ways to impress your clients during a business meal.
- Book the perfect romantic meal.
- Foods to avoid during a business lunch.
- The most popular way to propose over dinner.
- The perfect length for a dinner speech.

4. A Honey Farmer

How many honey brands do you see on the shelf at your local grocery store? Make a mental note next time you go shopping. Other than slight flavor nuances, customers choose honey based on price and branding. As a honey farmer, what can you do to build your reputation and gain loyalty?

Here's a start to a great series of information about honey:

- Ten health benefits of raw honey.
- The healing properties of honey.
- Little known facts about the humble honey bee.
- An old-fashioned honey and ginger flu remedy.

- Teaching your children to be safe around bees.
- Five homemade honey face packs.
- How to disinfect a wound with honey.
- Myths about the honey bee.

Add to this the almost unending list of recipes, health and beauty tips using honey and you'll have more than enough to keep your messages flowing.

5. A Teacher

Independent training and teaching is a very competitive niche. Reputation and word of mouth are vital when you want to stand out from the crowd.

Here are a few examples of topics that a music teacher could use to build a reputation as an expert.

- The benefits of music for child development.
- Ten surprising ways that music affects the brain.
- How to pick the best study music.
- Health benefits of music.
- How to tell if your child is musically gifted.
- You're never too old to learn to play an instrument.

These are just six suggestions of an endless list of valuable topics that could be covered.

So far we've looked at the concept of content and what it can do for your business. We've also taken a look at what could be considered as valuable content for five sample businesses. It's clear that we need good quality content and lots of it. The question now is: how do you keep up with the demand for fresh content?

4 KEEPING UP WITH THE DEMAND

How to keep up with the demand for fresh content

We've looked at why you need good content to draw people to your business, and why you need lots of it to remain relevant on the internet.

What options do you have in terms of keeping up with the content demand? There are only three real options:

- do it yourself
- outsource or delegate
- buy ready-made content

Do it yourself

You can take the do-it-yourself approach and create content from scratch. Writing the content yourself takes a lot of time, and time is a luxury in any small business. You will need the time to research, write and edit your content until the article is ready. The problem is that if you don't enjoy writing, it's not one of your strengths or if you are short on time then creating quality content can be a real problem.

Outsourcing or delegating

On the other hand, there are some options for outsourcing your content creations. You can:

- hire a full-time employee to produce content

- ask a current staff member to pick up the task
- hire a freelancer as and when needed

The first two options are seldom possible when your business is still small - and is impossible when you've chosen to run your business on your own. An easy solution is to hire an outsider to produce your content for you. This may save you time but will end up costing you a lot in the long run. A writer will charge you full price for your articles, which will vary depending on whom you've hired. When you need a continuous flow of content, this will work out to be a costly solution.

Buy ready-made content

The third option is to buy cost effective, ready-made articles that come with full editing and ownership rights so that you can use them as you see fit. As mentioned before, this type of content is called Private Label Rights or PLR content.

In the introduction to this book, I mentioned how and why I got into the PLR business. In the spirit of full disclosure, I want to point out that there are many PLR providers who sell their writing on the internet. If you choose to buy content, be sure to take some time to choose the best provider for your business.

We'll look at what to consider when choosing good PLR in a moment. But first, let's look at an explanation of PLR, how it will benefit you and the typical usage rights associated with PLR writing.

PART 2
PRIVATE LABEL RIGHTS

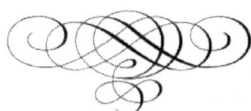

SAY MORE BY DOING LESS

5 AN INTRODUCTION TO PRIVATE LABEL RIGHTS

What is Private Label Rights writing?

Private Label Rights (PLR) is content written by someone else who then sells you ready made articles with the rights to edit and use it as you wish. One PLR article is sold to multiple buyers. This makes it possible for the writer to charge a lower price than if they were selling an article exclusively to one customer.

Each PLR supplier sells their customers different rights as part of the purchase. Most of the time you can edit the information as you please - break it apart, combine it with other resources, rewrite it completely or simply adapt it to meet your needs. You can even repurpose it into completely different formats such as audio, video or graphics. The great thing about PLR is that you have the right to rebrand the information as if you wrote it yourself. This means that you don't have to give the original writer any public credit. It is as if you are the original author. In the second half of the book, we'll look at the thirty different ways to take a written article with PLR rights and use it as the basis of your content marketing message.

PLR is generally sold in a written format but there are also suppliers that sell PLR graphics, audio, video or software that can be rebranded as your own. We'll be focusing on written PLR products.

Why should I consider using PLR content?

PLR writing is more cost effective than other outsourcing options. Because the costs are kept low, you would be able to afford to buy a number of articles for the same price you would pay for a single, exclusive article. This will help with your supply of continuous information to the public.

It also has the time saving benefits when compared to writing your own content. Since the article is pre-written, you save the time that you would have spent researching, writing and editing the content if you had written it yourself. All you need to do is spend a few minutes customizing the content. A well written article should only take on average ten minutes to customize.

The minimum modification you need to do is addition of the keywords you want to show up in an internet search, as well as the personal touches and nuances to match it to your individual style of writing and to add a reference to your business. You might want to spend a bit more time if you choose to add researched facts specific to your own geography or niche. But generally the article will only need a few modifications before you can use it. You'll need to allocate more time if you choose to adapt the information into a completely different format, but even then, having the pre-written article as a foundation saves you a great deal of time.

A good PLR writer puts the same amount of effort and quality into writing a PLR article as they would into writing an exclusive article for a client. If you choose the right PLR provider then you will not need to worry about content quality.

Once you've purchased a PLR article, you can use it as many times as you would like and in as many formats as your license allows. It's a great shortcut to producing content.

Rights / Licenses

When you purchase PLR content it will come with a license which describes your rights as the buyer. Your license will be sent to you in the article itself or as a separate file in your download. This file is typically called "Read Me", "Read Me First" or "Rights". It is extremely important to read this file and understand how you are permitted to change and reuse the content. If you are in any doubt, contact the supplier of the content and simply ask them for clarity. This will help you protect yourself from any type of copyright infringements later on.

Although PLR licenses are usually very generous, purchasing content does not always allow you to use it as you see fit. Certain licenses will have restrictions attached to them, while others allow you to do anything with the content.

Here is a list of the most frequent license agreements that PLR writers use, along with the explanation of each. Each provider will choose which to apply to their products.

License rights	Explanation
[yes] you can claim to be the author	This is always a core right to PLR.
[yes] or [no] you can/cannot edit this content completely	On occasion, a writer will allow you to rebrand the information as your own but will not allow you to customize the content in any way. This is usually because they have included links to their own products or services in the article. If this is the case, it will generally be disclosed to you before you buy the content. When you buy PLR with no editing rights then you simply rebrand the content

License rights	Explanation
	with your business branding but keep the information as is.
[yes] or [no] you can/cannot translate this into any language	There will only be a restriction on this right if the information cannot be applied to a specific geography or culture. Usually full translation is allowed.
[yes] or [no] you can/cannot insert information about your products, services or affiliate links	If you choose to add product information or affiliate links, make sure that you have the appropriate permissions from your list to market to them.
[yes] or [no] you can/cannot repurpose this product	This right will point out the extent to which you are allowed to turn the text into other formats.
The following rights specify restrictions to the price at which you could offer the final product to your audience.	
[yes] or [no] you can/cannot give away the products you create with this content OR Product must be resold at a minimum of $xx	In some cases PLR providers don't want to create the impression that their content has a low monetary value and so they specify a minimum price that the end product must be sold for. This is not a very common specification for individual articles. It may be applied when you buy PLR which may not be edited because it refers to a third party product or service which holds a specific value.
[yes] or [no] you may/may not sell this product in a dime sale	A dime sale is a type of promotion where a seller sets a very low sale price initially. This price then increase by one US dime with each sale made until it reaches the original product price. The sooner you buy, the cheaper the

License rights	Explanation
	product is. Some PLR providers prohibit this because it devalues the product. Once again, it shouldn't apply to individual articles which are usually not resold anyway.
The next collection specifies which rights (if any) you can pass on to your customers when you distribute the content to them:	
[yes] or [no] you can/cannot use this content as website content	This restriction is introduced to protect your rankings. Using the content as-is will affect your ranking because Google will identify it as duplicated content already used by other PLR buyers. Some PLR providers will request a degree of customization before using the content on your website for the exact same protection. Limiting the number of sales per article will also help protect your rankings.
[yes] or [no] you can/cannot resell this content as is	Most PLR providers will not allow you to resell the content in the same format that you've bought it.
[YES] or [no] You can/cannot sell Resell Rights	If you are given the rights to resell the content, you will need to be clear about whether or not your customer is able to resell it as well. When you pass on resell rights you give your own customers the right to resell the content.
[yes] or [NO] You can/cannot sell Master Resell Rights	Master Resell Rights means that your customers and their customers can resell the content. There is no restriction on who is allowed to resell or how many times they can resell.

License rights	Explanation
[yes] or [no] you can/cannot pass on Private Label Rights to your audience	This means that your customers do or do not have the right to rebrand the information as their own or distribute under their own names in any way - regardless of whether you sell or give the end product to them.

A PLR writer will probably only use a few of these rights. As an example, here's what you will receive when you buy one of our CustomWrite™ PLR articles from The Communication Shop:

- [Yes] you can edit this content completely
- [Yes] you can rebrand your customized content and claim to be the author
- [No] you may not name "TheCommunicationShop.com" or "Belinda Cuthbert" as the author
- [Yes] you can translate this article into any language
- [Yes] you may insert information about your own products, services or affiliate links provided you have the correct permission to market to your audience
- [Yes] you can sell or giveaway the information products you create with this content
- [No] you cannot distribute or resell this article in its original format. Only customized information products created using this article may be sold and distributed.
- [Yes] you can repurpose this information into any content format
- [Yes] you can add this content to both paid or free membership sites once customized
- [No] you may not use this content as website content "as is" until you have changed at least 30% of the content. This is for your own ranking benefit.
- [No] you may not pass on Private Label Rights to your audience. In other words, you may not give your

audience/customers the right to put their own name on the products you create using this information. You may give them the rights to distribute or resell your products but you, or the business you represent, must remain the author of the content.

The bottom line is that each PLR seller uses a different set of rights. Read and understand your license rights before you begin working with the content to avoid any copyright infringements.

SAY MORE BY DOING LESS

PART 3
GROWING YOUR GRAND WITH PLR

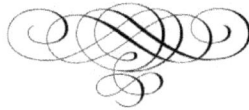

SAY MORE BY DOING LESS

6 DEALING WITH DUPLICATE CONTENT

Does your credibility suffer when you use the same content as other buyers?

There's nothing ethically wrong with publishing a piece of PLR writing without having made any changes. You purchased the rights to use it and, unless your license states otherwise, you can publish it without any customization. Having said that, there are two main reasons why I believe that customizing your PLR is the right thing to do.

Firstly, search engines penalize you when they consider your content to be the same, or too similar, to that of another website. This affects your rankings. Customizing your content will improve the position of your site during a search. Ranking is less of a concern when you use the PLR in eBooks, giveaway reports, video, audio or graphic since search engines don't monitor these as a ranking factor.

Secondly, and the most important reason in my mind, is if you want to be considered an expert in your own right then it's important to put your personal stamp on the information. Just because you bought content doesn't mean that you don't have any thoughts of your own. This is an opportunity for you to show your customers what you know and feel about your field. Be passionate, add examples from your business, use case studies, recommend products or solutions and add your own personality to the message. Customers want to hear from you. This is a chance to build rapport.

At The Communication Shop we add editing suggestions to our CustomWrite™ PLR articles to recommend ways in which our customers can customize our content. Regardless of who you buy your PLR from, it's important to make it your own.

If you are worried that your information isn't unique enough, then refer to our downloadable resource guide where we will tell you about an online tools that can show you which parts of your content is considered to be duplicated elsewhere on the web. You can easily target this duplicate wording and make a few small changes until it is unique.

Will people notice that you're using the same content as other buyers?

As a writer, my first impression of PLR was that it "just isn't right" to sell the same article to more than one customer. When I write exclusive freelance material for customers, I always do my research from scratch and I don't repeat information used in a previous assignment. My writing ethics probably made me the most skeptical person when it came to considering PLR as a form of content. Until I thought it through logically.

I'll use our CustomWrite™ PLR as an example to illustrate my point.

At The Communication Shop, I only sell an article a maximum of 250 times. Once the 250 licenses are sold out, I remove the article from the website forever.

Of the 250 available licenses we know that not all will be bought in the same month. Sometimes sales can happen over the course of a year or two, depending on the popularity of the topic. This means that there are never 250 customers preparing to send the same piece of information out to their audience simultaneously.

For argument's sake, let's say that 100 people have purchased the same article in one month - which is unlikely - but we'll stick with the number to make the point.

Of those 100 buyers, not all of them will choose to use the content in a written format on the internet. Some may choose to use it in offline marketing, some on their web page, others will use it in their eBook, or social media while the rest repurpose it into graphics, video or audio products. Some customers may not even use it in the month that they bought it. This severely limits the chances that customers will identify the content as being duplicated.

Add to this the fact that the 100 buyers are spread out geographically (in our case globally) which means that they don't likely share any audience members on their marketing lists.

Even if all 100 buyers DO decide to use the article on the internet, in a written format, during the same month, the chances of one internet visitor coming across the same information twice is minuscule because of the sheer volume of information available on the internet.

I'd like to quote some stats from Royal Pingdom to illustrate the size of the internet based audience. The stats are based on 2012 measurements and were posted by Royal Pingdom in January 2013. Visit the link in our reference section to see the full list of stats. (Royal Pingdom)[iv]

For our purposes, we want to share these particular numbers to illustrate the vastness of the internet:

- 2.4 billion – Number of Internet users worldwide
- 634 million – Number of total websites on the internet
- 51 million – Number of websites added during 2012 alone
- 87.8 million – Number of Tumblr blogs
- 59.4 million – Number of WordPress blog sites around the world
- 144 billion – Total emails sent per day worldwide
- 1 billion – Number of monthly active users on

Facebook

- 2.7 billion – Number of likes on Facebook every day
- 200 million – Monthly active users on Twitter
- 175 million – Average number of tweets sent every day throughout 2012
- 187 million – Number of members on LinkedIn
- 135 million – Number of monthly active users on Google+
- 5 billion – How many times per day the +1 button on Google+ is used
- 1.2 trillion – Number of searches on Google in 2012
- 1.3 billion – Number of smart phones in use worldwide by end of 2012
- 59% – Share of global mobile data traffic that was video
- 14 million – Number of Vimeo users
- 200 petabytes – Amount of video played on Vimeo during 2012 (1 petabyte = 1 thousand million million bytes)
- 4 billion – Number of hours of video watched on YouTube per month
- 60 million – Number of global viewers monthly on Ustream

These statistics are astounding and illustrate the massive amount of information housed on the internet. There is an immeasurably small chance that your customer will see the same information, used by two different businesses, at the same time.

Of course the main reason you don't need to worry about duplicate content is still this...you'll be customizing your information anyway - because your voice is important.

7 WHAT TO CONSIDER WHEN CHOOSING A PLR PROVIDER

Not all PLR is created equal. It's worthwhile doing some homework before buying your content. Here's what to look out for.

Article release and review dates

Look for a release or review date on the PLR content. PLR writers generally try to ensure that articles will not become outdated too quickly but it is wise to check when they were written. Some PLR with unlimited resell rights tend to make their way around for years and could be outdated by the time you come across the offer.

There are some topics that will not easily become outdated, for example "The healing properties of honey" or "How to choose the right wine to compliment your dinner". There are, however, topics where the factual content can become outdated very quickly. These include topics that discuss technology or product reviews. For example "The best option for a 7" tablet" or "This year's favorite family car". You can only decide if the article is still relevant if you know when it was written or at least reviewed.

Use your discretion based on the topic and look for a date if you are concerned.

Number of licenses available

Some PLR providers sell an article a limited number of times while others offer unlimited licenses.

For example, one provider may only sell their "How to set New Year's resolutions" a maximum of 300 times while another provider may not limit the number of sales at all.

The fewer licenses available, the fewer people will own and use the content and the more valuable that content will be to a PLR buyer. We've already discussed the vastness of the internet and how to avoid duplication. However, limited licenses do minimize the risk of posting duplicate content.

Writing quality

Occasionally you will come across poorly written PLR which may have been written by a non-English speaker or it may be content that was created by putting an article through "spinning" software. This type of software automatically makes changes to content and creates a slightly different version. The quality of writing that has gone through such a program is never guaranteed unless the PLR provider has checked it for errors. Unfortunately, this isn't always done and often comes out with a mechanical feel or containing grammatical errors. In both cases you may be disappointed with the quality and will spend more time correcting the content than is worth your time.

Try to determine the typical quality of the writer before buying content from them. Most PLR providers offer a few free articles on their site so that you can see the quality of their writing. Others give you a sneak peak at the articles on the website. Customer reviews are also a great way to see if previous customers have been satisfied or not.

Price

Be very careful when receiving offers to buy PLR for a ridiculously low price. For example, buying 100 articles for a total of $1 should give you an indication that the quality is either questionable or that the content is outdated or overused.

Most PLR providers offer great specials from time to time where you can snag a bargain. Your concern should be about buying from PLR providers whose prices are continuously too good to be true. Always do a due diligence check if you're not sure.

Keep in mind that when you buy from a credible PLR provider, you have in essence outsourced your content to a professional writer or niche expert. The writer is taking a risk in providing the content at such a low price since there is no guarantee that they will sell enough articles to cover the initial resource costs of producing it. You will therefore find that credible writers therefore charge an affordable yet realistic fee for their effort.

Packs or Individual

Many PLR providers group their articles according to topic and sell them in packs for one overall price. Other providers post their articles individually allowing buyers to choose as many or as few as necessary from a selection of topics. Both have their advantages.

Packs are wonderful if you want more than one article on a related topic. The price often works out cheaper per unit than if you were buying articles individually which makes them good value for money. The writer will give you a list of headings so that you have a good idea what you're buying. If you choose to buy packs, consider whether or not you need all the articles. If you don't think you'll use them all then decide if you're willing to pay the package price for the number of articles you know you will use. Before you buy, check to see if all the articles in the pack will apply to your audience. The information in some articles are prepared for a specific country, for example packs on choosing retirement benefits, investments, housing investment etc. This is usually quite easy to establish by looking at the article titles.

When articles are sold individually you have the convenience of choosing the exact articles that you need without the risk of buying unnecessary information. This allows you to mix and match topics from a variety of subjects to meet your needs or just to buy one at a time as you need them. Choosing a unique combination of articles gives you an exponentially greater chance of producing a 100% unique end product when you start combining articles into eBooks, blog series, training courses, video series etc.

Both approaches have their benefits and your preference will become obvious when you consider your needs.

8 CUSTOMIZING YOUR FIRST PLR ARTICLE

It all starts with one written article...and grows from there

Now that you've bought some PLR, it's time to put the content to good use. We'll start off by looking at how you can customize and use a single article.

Customizing PLR may seem daunting if you don't consider yourself a writer, but since the majority of the composition (or crafting) has been done for you, you can think of this step as "tweaking" or "personalizing" rather than rewriting.

Let's take the customization section by section.

Heading

Your heading should grab your reader's attention. You'll want to reconstruct the heading so that it represents exactly what you want your customers to hear. It needs to tell readers what to expect in the article. Build in keywords that you think your customers will use in their internet search so that Google can index the information correctly.

For example, the PLR writer may have used a heading such as:

Sleeping habits of successful students

You could tweak this to be something like:

- Five ways that sleep can improve your studies
- Why all nighters won't get you an A
- Good grades need good sleep

The more accurate your heading is, the greater the chance that your information will pop up when readers do an internet search. Don't use vague headings like, "Wakey, wakey sleepy head" or "Slumber Success". It doesn't tell your reader anything about the content of the article and Google won't understand where you want to be indexed.

My personal favorite when rewriting a heading is to rephrase it as a question. This speaks directly to the question or problem that the reader has in mind then they search for information and it also implies that the article will present them with a solution. For example:

- How will good sleeping habits improve my grades?
- Can sufficient sleep help me get through high school?
- Does my child need extra sleep during exam time?

These types of headings imply that you're offering more than just useful information; you're offering an answer to the readers question.

We've just come up with six alternatives to our original article heading. Make changes to your PLR headings until you're comfortable that they reflect what you have to say to readers.

Introduction

The introduction is a great place to add some personality to the article. I find the easiest way to write an introduction is to ask myself the question: "Why am I writing this message to my audience and why now?"

Let's go back to the article about sleep.

The PLR article you purchase may give you an introductory

sentence that reads:

"Developing good sleeping patterns is important at the school going age. Good sleeping habits can help students cope with the stress of writing exams."

However, you have a reason and context for wanting to share this message with your readers. You understand why you want to send a message and why you're sending it at this particular point in time. So your introduction could look something like this:

"With High School exams just around the corner I am sure there are many stressed parents and anxious students. I know a little secret that I want to share with you and it's about how good sleep patterns can help your child handle the pressure of exam time."

Let's use a second example. You may have bought an article on preparing garden soil for the planting season. The PLR introduction could have been something like:

"Good soil preparation will help to prolong the life of your spring flowers."

You could customize it to say:

"I'm so excited to think that we're already half way through the winter season. Although the weather is still icy outside, it's time to start planning our spring planting. There's a lot we can do to prepare the soil so that it's ready to receive our spring seedlings and prolong the life of our spring flowers."

Alternatively, if you're not too keen on rewriting the paragraph you can simply add in a few words and some context of your own.

"Spring is just around the corner and we know that good

soil preparation will help to prolong the life of our spring blooms. That's exactly what we're going to focus on this week."

In all our examples, we simply added a bit of context to infuse a bit more context and personality into the introduction.

If you're nervous about rewriting your PLR then turn to our resource guide in which we share some resources that will make it easier to change your article. These are great for replacing words with appropriate synonyms, and that also helps to add your own voice to the article.

The body of the article

Here are some tips on how to personalize the body of the article:

- Replace words that you seldom personally use with words you are more comfortable with.
- Replace foreign sounding words with local variances. If you are aiming your message only at a local audience then use the words that they are more likely to use in conversation.

For example - when writing to a South African audience, you would replace the word "barbeque" with "braai" or "gas" with "petrol". Make your article as easy to read as possible. So, ditch the words that your audience wouldn't be familiar with.

- When a point or statement is made, add an example from your personal experience to back it up.
- When a fact is stated, support it with a local statistic or research that you've read.
- If you're providing a list of tips, tell the reader which one has worked well for you and your customers. You can also add more tips to the list or replace one or two with some that you prefer.

For example, "Why not try all five tips to help you get a better night's sleep. I personally found that number three was a winner when my son was writing his exams."

- Another way to easily customize the body is to change the structure of a sentence by combining two short sentences or splitting a particularly long sentence. Alternatively, try paraphrasing a sentence to change the style.

You'll find that your article will start looking more unique simply by making a few changes.

Product promotions

Some articles lend themselves nicely to promoting products or service related to the topic. This should only be done occasionally since your intention is to build your brand through free information. However, there are times when promotions won't appear intrusive.

If your article deals with a particular topic and you either know of, or provide, a great product or service to benefit the reader, then it is possible to incorporate these details with a link to a sales page. This could be a product of your own, an affiliate product or simply a product you've used and would like to recommend without necessary receiving any compensation.

I cannot stress enough that you have to obtain the right permissions from your list before you market to them. Further, you need to make sure that all product recommendations are legally sound. There are many restrictions particularly when it comes to promoting health related products.

Product recommendations should be few and far between and should only be used if you think that the product is a beneficial option for the reader. You don't only have to refer to products. You may also want to refer readers to further information that you've found useful.

Closing paragraph

Round off the article by encouraging your reader to apply the information. For example:

> "I really hope that you're just as excited as I am about preparing your garden for spring. You'll appreciate the extra time you've put in when you start seeing the benefits of your hard work as those first blossoms appear. Happy gardening."

OR

> "Raising a child can be difficult, especially when they are stressed about something like exams. I hope that the tips I've given you today have provided you with some ideas to help your child alleviate exam pressure by adopting good sleeping habits. Here's to your child's successful studies."

Prompt for further contact

The closing paragraph can also be used as a prompt for the reader to contact you if they need any help implementing the solution that was discussed. Let's use the same examples from above but add a call to action.

> "I really hope that you're just as excited as I am about preparing your garden for spring. You'll appreciate the extra time you've put in when you start seeing the benefits of your hard work as those first blossoms appear.
>
> We've just unpacked an amazing range of soil supplements and gardening equipment. Please pop by our store if you need to stock up. You'll find us at *street address*. It will be our pleasure to assist you. Or give us a call on *your contact number* if you need advice. We'll be happy to help.
>
> Happy gardening."

OR

> " Raising a child can be difficult, especially when they are

stressed about something like exams. I hope that the tips I've given you today have provided you with some ideas to help your child alleviate exam pressure by adopting good sleeping habits.

Consider attending one of our "Strong Parent, Strong Child" workshops if you're ever feeling overwhelmed. You'll find a schedule on our website at *your website name*. Sometimes you just need some extra support when the going gets tough.

Here's to your child's success."

We include a detailed guide to customizing these components with every PLR sale at The Communication Shop. You can download this guide as part of your free bonus material. Simply log onto www.thecommunicationshop.com and request your bonus under the tab "Say More by Doing Less".

BELINDA CUTHBERT

9 USING YOUR CUSTOMIZED ARTICLE

Time to put your article to good use

At this point you would have customized your first PLR article. This article now becomes the basis for the 30 different uses we've been referring to throughout the book.

We'll start off by looking at how to use your customized article with minimal further changes.

Write blog posts (1)

You can now create a blog post from your customized article.

A blog is a personal web page that features the blogger's views, experiences, observation and their expertise. It is a great way to keep in touch with your audience and get feedback from them at the same time.

There are three main things that distinguish blog writing from other types of online writing.

1) A blog post generally includes the writers personal views on the topic.

2) Blogs allow readers an opportunity to respond to the writer through online comments.

3) The writing style is both conversational and informative, creating the feeling that there is a connection between the writer and reader.

Blogging is easy to do and could cost nothing is you choose to use one of the free blogging platforms available. The most popular blogging platform today is WordPress which not only gives you the option of a free blog, but the ability to build all necessary pages for a full website. If you already have a website and just want to add a blog then create one separately and interlink the two. Incorporating a blog on your website is the easiest way to turn a static site into a dynamic one which improves your search rankings.

Creating blog posts

Use your customized article as the body of your blog post. It will only need a bit of tweaking to give it a more personal style if you choose.

Read through your customized article to make sure it is conversational enough and that you have added your own views to the existing content.

The recommended length of a blog is between 300 and 500 words but if it's well written and packed with information then you could stretch it to a maximum of 1000 words. The word processor you're using will do an automatic word count for you. If you have a lot to say and don't want to exceed the 500 word mark, then split your blog into two shorter articles and publish them as a series.

Blogging frequency

Blogging on a regular basis will help Google index your site faster and you will start attracting more visitors. Be realistic about how often you will be able to prepare your blog posts before committing a frequency to yourself or your readers.

The frequency of your blog depends on how visible you want to be to your audience and to Google. If your blog is the primary connection with customers, then you should blog frequently, up to a few times per week. A down side to this approach is that you are only connecting with the audience that enjoys blogs which may exclude people that prefer other types of social media. Too many blogs may also come across as overbearing and cost you your audience. A better strategy is to schedule fewer blog posts and interlace these with messages on other social media.

Preferably blog once a week to stay top of mind, but at least once a month as a minimum if you find you can't manage more than that.

Whatever frequency you decide on, make a decision and stick to it. Being consistent is better than starting off strong and fading as time goes by.

You can save time by preparing a number of posts upfront and then scheduling them to publish automatically on predetermined dates. You can set aside time once a month for example to customize a few articles and then set them on autopilot to free you up to focus on your business. Then you'll only need to free up the time to respond to comments as they come through with each new post.

Create Website content (2)

Preparing website content is different to a preparing a blog post. Web content is geared towards giving visitors as much information about your business as possible. These factual pages tend to be quite one directional with some contact forms if viewers wish to contact you for further information. You website is therefore mainly a marketing tool telling people who you are and why they should buy from you. The pages remain relatively static unless you make significant changes to your business or its products.

So how can you use PLR to populate your website? PLR articles obviously won't contain information about your specific business, however, it will help to fill the pages that give viewers more information about the industry you've chosen to be in.

Let's say you're a music teacher wanting to attract students through your website.

You wouldn't use PLR for the "About us" or "Contact us" or "See our music schedule" pages. The PLR is not specific enough for that.

But you would be able to use PLR for information pages that show viewers why music is important and why they would benefit from using your services. You could use PLR to create pages such as "What music can do for you", "Why everyone should learn to play an instrument", "Frequently asked questions about music", "The history of instruments", or a "Did you know" text box onto your home page. This shows your visitors that you have a great deal of knowledge about your field and that you're willing to share information.

Produce Online newsletters (3)

Almost everything that people choose to do online occurs faster than their offline variations. This includes the amount of time that someone will allocate to reading an article online as opposed to offline.

It's therefore important to keep online writing short and to the point. Use more keywords and less "filler content" than you would for offline writing. Keep this in mind when preparing your online newsletter.

Online newsletters are used to give readers important information, quickly and concisely, and then allow them to move onto the next piece of online content. Your time with them is limited.

How to use your PLR

Review your customized PLR article. Remove any unnecessary phrases or words that are simply used as a filler. Of course, you'll need to make sure that the sentences still make sense once you've removed whatever you feel is unnecessary. Make sure your sentences are short and that each one makes an important point. Shorten your paragraphs by paraphrasing if possible.

In essence, get rid of everything that's not necessary.

Produce Offline newsletters (4)

Offline newsletters on the other hand, still contain an element of reading pleasure. You can get away with longer sentences and more descriptive content than you would when writing for the internet.

Readers are willing to give more time to each article mainly because you usually don't need to finish it in one go. Think of the time that you spend reading a magazine or newspaper as opposed to reading an online newsletter or news site. You tend to be in a more relaxed environment and more open to information when you take the time to read a printed publication. If you don't finish an article immediately, you always have the chance of going back. If you're reading an online newsletter, you tend to open it once and don't return once you've closed the link. Another factor is that online information sites are filled with links and once you've clicked off the page you are not very likely to return. Your readers have this exact experience when they are reading so take advantage of being able to provide a little bit more in offline information.

How to use your PLR

Use these factors to your advantage by taking your customized PLR and adding some readership enjoyment. Be descriptive. Expand on examples, tell your story and draw the reader in with additional information. Add a human element and emotional connection that you would not easily have been able to do in an online newsletter.

Place a Local Newspaper Educational (5)

Community newspapers are often prepared to publish educational articles that add value to their communities. Contact the editor of your local newspaper to find out if they would be interested in free, interesting information that will add value to their audience.

How to use your PLR

Use your customized PLR article as the basis of your newspaper article. Try to localize the information you've bought by referring to the local geography or local statistics in some way. Consider what would be important in the newspapers area of distribution and then provide readers with the information. Make sure that all your original facts are applicable to the specialized audience. Use local statistics, case studies, community examples or simple references to the local economy.

Newspaper will usually not allow you to promote a product or service in an educational and so you will need to focus providing information to help readers solve a challenge or problem. The good news is that the newspaper will credit you as the author and will generally place your name and contact details alongside the content. Your reputation will be boosted, and you will gain exposure in the local community.

Use Direct Mailing (6)

Another way to reach your local audience is through direct mailing or post office drops.

Provide useful information to your community by printing pamphlets and mailing them to your marketing list or dropping them off at your local mail distribution points. Countries have different regulations regarding direct mailing so first make sure that you are within your legal rights before you use this approach.

How to use your PLR

Since printing and distribution costs are relatively high, we recommend that you make good use of the opportunity to make some money off the method. Prepare your information in a similar informative tone as you did for the newspaper educational, but this time use the opportunity to promote your business and tell the customer what you can sell them to help solve the problem you're addressing. Make sure that the information is comprehensive enough to add value whether they choose to buy from you or not. Customers who take the time to read your mailer should be rewarded with good information.

Place Advertorials (7)

Print advertising is another important aspect of business that every owner needs particularly to market to one's local market.

Not all media will be open to placing your information in their publication free of charge. If you have an advertising budget then consider placing an advertorial or infomercial in local publications. An advertorial is a branded piece of information. The main goal is to build your brand by providing great information. Because you pay for the space, you are able to brand the information with any contact details you choose to place.

You will need a graphic designer to create a good design. Use the designer you use for all your other design jobs or take a look at our recommendation on our resource page. You'll also need someone to proofread your advertorial to make sure that it is 100% correct before placing it in the public space. The editor of your local newspaper would have picked up any errors before printing your media publication, but advertorials are usually published in the exact form that you submit to the publication. That means it's wise to have someone proofread it first. Ask someone you know who has a good command of written English or submit is to a specialist. Our resource page also recommends some options.

Engage in Guest Blogging (8)

A popular way to reach new audiences is to write a guest post for someone else's blog. It's the internet equivalent of writing a guest column for your favorite magazine.

Do a search for blogs related to your niche but not in direct competition to your own business. Choose a blogger that you respect and whose discussion topic is complimentary to your own. Contact them through a private message and ask if they'll allow you to write an article for their blog. The host will usually first take a look at your current website and online profile to see if there is a good fit from both sides. Their reputation is at stake if they post poor quality guest posts or if they associate themselves with someone who has a poor reputation.

The benefit of guest blogging is that you will have exposure to the host blogger's existing marketing list. The host will usually allow you to post a link back to your own website or blog at the end of the post. If the host's list has enjoyed reading your point of view, then some will possibly sign up as a subscriber to your list. It's also common practice to offer the host's list a great discount on one of your products, but check that your host is comfortable with this first. The guest post, therefore, has the potential to increase your list and possibly make immediate sales.

Being accepted as a guest will increase your authority because it shows that you are considered worthy of writing for others. Your credibility will also increase because when people Google your name, they will see that you are associated with other online personalities.

How to use your PLR

One of the general conditions if you're accepted as a guest blogger is that you will not use content that you've used in your own blog or other online publications before. In this case simply buy and customize a PLR article that you haven't used before. Another option is to combine the best extracts of your previously customized PLR articles and create a great new, unique one. Just take all the main points from each article and combine them in a conversational tone. Include a new image and a link back to your main blog and website.

Although you should always make sure that your blog posts are top quality, it is especially important to make sure guest posts are top-notch. Both your, and the host's reputation is at stake. If the host enjoyed working with you then, you might be invited to come back for more guest posts. Return the favor and ask them if they would like to guest blog for you. This way they will have exposure to your list and you will have one less blog post to write.

Be sure to honor any conditions that the host asks of you. If you send them an article that doesn't meet their standards then they simply won't post it.

Use Autoresponder sequences / Automated emails (9)

Gone are the days when a small business owner had to manually send out promotional or customer relations emails in batches until everyone on their list had received the message. Today there is an impressive list of autoresponder services that can help you put email distribution tasks on autopilot.

Think of messages like product promotions, a note welcoming someone onto your list, a link to a free download, holiday greetings, store renovation announcements, or a coupon code when you're feeling especially generous. An autoresponder allows you to upload your list to their service and then pre-schedule emails that need to go out on a specific day. Most autoresponders also allow you to design a professional looking email and send it out from your business email address.

This frees up your time to run your business instead of worrying about marketing emails.

How you can use PLR

Let's use our restaurant owner as an example and assume that they have an account with an autoresponder service.

The first thing your autoresponder provides is the ability to create your own squeeze page to use on your website, Facebook page or even in an email. A squeeze page is a web form that asks the visitor to enter their name and email address - usually in return for a gift. It is also referred to as an "opt in form". An autoresponder not only allows you to create the squeeze page but will also capture and store the information of everyone who completes the form. This becomes part of your existing marketing list.

For the sake of this example let's say that our restaurant owner has created a squeeze page for their website that reads:

> "We'd like treat you to 50% discount on your next meal with us. Complete the form and we'll email you a discount code. We'll also start sending you great information and details about upcoming specials."

When a visitor fills out the form, they will receive a confirmation email (sent to them by your autoresponder). This confirmation email will ask their permission to have their email address added to your mailing list. When they click on the confirmation link, the autoresponder adds them to your list, and they will begin receiving the pre-scheduled marketing messages that you would have scheduled into the service.

The restaurant owner may have added these messages in the autoresponder sequence:
1) [date of opt in] - Here is your coupon code. We look forward to seeing you at *restaurant name*
2) [2 days later] - How to select the best wine to complement your meal (content marketing)
3) [1 week later] - Food to avoid when you're on a date (content marketing)
4) [1 week later] - New menu choices at *restaurant name* (product promotion)
5) [1 week later] - How to impress your boss during a business meal. (content marketing)

And so it continues. All the messages are pre-scheduled. If a customer joins your list on 1 January, the sequence will commence from that day. If they join on 15 June, that same sequence will commence from that date. And it's all automated.

Another option is to send a broadcast messages to your entire list on one day regardless of when they joined. For example, you could plan a message for 20 January that reads "Don't wait until it's too late to make your Valentine's Day reservations". This will be sent out to your entire list on 20 January regardless of where they are in the pre-scheduled sequence.

Some autoresponders may have slightly different features, but this is the general process.

How to prepare your autoresponder emails

Email messages should be approximately 300 words in length - no more. The most time effective way to set up a sequence is to buy a number of PLR articles, set a few hours aside to customize them, extract a concise 300 word message from each one and then set them up in your sequence where they are ready for the "autopilot" to step in.

You could schedule content for the next 3 months, 6 months or even 1 year in advance - this depends entirely on you. Book time in your diary about one month before your autoresponder is due to run out of messages. Repeat the process using new PLR articles. That way, the first people that joined the list will have a continued flow of messages.

Translate your purchase into any other language (10)

The final "gateway" to reaching your customer is to translate your end products into any other language suitable to your audience. If your audience is not fluent in English then why not communicate with them in their mother tongue?

Similarly why not add content that is specific to your audience geography if you are choosing to communicate with a specific location. For example, if you own a localized newspaper or publication and you want to point out the health advantages of outdoor living, then recommend special outdoor locations in close proximity. You can take this one step further and negotiate a special discount for your readers with the establishments you are marketing. Adding this type of value to your readers goes a long way in winning their hearts.

Alternatively, simply translate the content as you customized it, without adding localized information.

Moving on to more significant changes

Until now, we've only been doing some rewriting, tweaking and basic customizing of our PLR article. It's time to look at the concept of "repurposing" our article.

10 REPURPOSING YOUR ARTICLE

Now we can take the transformation of our PLR further by changing the article more dramatically. This is referred to as "repurposing" as opposed to "rewriting".

Rewriting is simply the rephrasing of some parts of the article to reflect your own writing style and then adding your professional opinion, examples, statistics, case studies, recommendations of products or services etc.

Repurposing content turns the article into something completely different.

I love this quote by Dave Kerpen of Likeable Media and Author of Likeable Business and Likeable Social Media, (as quoted by Heidi Cohen on her website):

> Repurposed content is content that was once meant for one thing and with a little adjusting finds a new home or audience. (Heidi Cohen)[v]

In this next section, we'll look at how we can do a little more "adjusting" to produce something new.

Extracting snippets from the customized article

One of the easiest and fastest ways to create messages is to extract short, punchy sections from your customized PLR article and use these as the core of your message. Social media is a particularly useful platform on which to do so.

Social media

Social media is a collective label for many different categories of online social platforms each developed with its own purpose. You'll read different opinions from social media gurus about the types of social media but there are arguably five key types, categorized according to their main function:

- Blog sites (which we discussed in the previous section)
- Social networking sites
- Bookmarking sites
- Social news sites
- Online discussion forums
- Media sharing sites

Social Networking Sites

A social networking site is an online location where a visitor is able to connect with a group with whom they have something in common. They either share common social circles, a profession, background or have similar interests. There is a connection that results in you sharing information with each other.

According to eBiz MBA, the top three social networking sites as at February 2014 were listed as:

- Facebook with 900,000,000 estimated unique monthly visitors
- Twitter with 290,000,000 estimated unique monthly visitors
- LinkedIn with 250,000,000 estimated unique monthly visitors (eBiz MBA)[vi]

You can use your customized article to prepare messages for each of these networking sites. Your writing for each site will differ slightly.

Using PLR for Facebook (11)

With close to 1 Billion active visitors, you'll be sure to find a respectable number of individuals who will be interested in the information you have to offer.

But if you want to attract a great following, you'll need to pay attention to your writing. According to research carried out by Beth Belle Cooper of Buffer:

- A Facebook post of below 250 characters can get 60% more interaction than posts that are longer than 250 characters. (Characters are the total number of letters, spaces and punctuation marks.)
- You can get up to 66% more interaction if you can keep your post under 80 characters. (Beth Belle Cooper)[vii]

This means that you must aim to keep your messages at less than 80 characters if possible, but never more than 250 characters, which is essentially only two or three short sentences.

Let's go back to our Honey Farmer example for a moment.

By now the Honey Farmer has customized his PLR and would like to extract some information to post on his Facebook fan page.

He wants to use the following paragraph from the customized article:

"I spend a great deal of time outdoors and, as a result, my hair and skin have taken serious strain. I had learnt to live with my damaged hair until I found out about the moisturizing properties of honey. I now add a teaspoon of honey to my daily quota of shampoo. You can mix the two together in your hand or a container before lathering. Try it for yourself. I do this with every wash and it's made a remarkable difference."

That paragraph is suitable for a blog post. Apart from being a useful piece of information, it is also descriptive and it contains your personal opinion and experience.

But it won't work as a Facebook post. By the time your visitor has read through the first sentence they're ready to move on to the next Facebook post.

If you apply the principle of 80 characters or less, then the fact should read something like this:

"Add a teaspoon of honey to your regular shampoo to smooth damaged hair." (72 Characters including spaces)

Here are some more examples:

- Rub raw honey on a wound to disinfect it and start the healing process. (74 characters including spaces)
- Moisturize dry skin patches by rubbing with honey and leaving for 30 min. (73 characters including spaces)
- Darker honey contains more minerals and nutrients than light colored honey. (75 characters including spaces)

Your customized PLR article contains a number of worthwhile facts and tips which can be used for short posts. Extract these points, paraphrase, take out all unnecessary words and keep the core meaning. Then post it onto Facebook.

The same principle of short and powerful sentences will apply to all social media in which the message only has a short onscreen lifespan. What I mean by this is that the message feed is continuously being updated which means that your message could be "bumped off" the viewing screen within the first hour or two.

Using PLR for Twitter (12)

Beth Belle Cooper's research[vi] also looked at the best length of a Tweet (Twitter message).

Similar to Facebook, Beth explains that shorter posts tend to enjoy more engagement on Twitter. The difference between a

Facebook and Twitter message is in with that fact that a Tweet should include a link to more online information or include a hash tag so that a subscriber can follow a similar discussion for more information.

Belle Cooper's research shows that the best length for a Tweet is between 120 and 130 characters. This includes the number of characters in the link or hash tag.

You can use the same facts you've extracted for your Facebook messages and then add your link or hash tag to the end, making sure the entire message is under 130 characters.

Don't post the same information on Facebook and Twitter simultaneously. Some of your followers will subscribe to both and you don't want to create the impression that one media is actually a duplicate of the other. Plan your distribution so that the facts are alternated between the two media to avoid simultaneous posts of the same fact.

The only exception is when your message is date sensitive, for example a message related to a particular holiday where the message needs to go out on all your social media on the same day. In this instance try to word the messages differently for each media so that they are not identical.

Buffer's research[vi] goes on to explain that you will apply different techniques to creating your Tweet depending on whether you are looking for re-tweets or for engagement.

- If you want your readers to re-tweet: You have 86% more chance of your message being re-tweeted when it includes a link and is under 130 characters long.

- If you want two way interaction: If you're looking for engagement then don't include a link and keep your message shorter - under 100 characters is optimal. This is because once someone clicks out of the original tweet using a link, they are not very likely to come back to engage. So save the links for re-tweets and the unlinked comments for engagement.

As with all the techniques in this book, I recommend that you keep your messages aligned to your core business and uphold the quality standards of your brand. Keep product marketing messages to a minimum and maximize content marketing. Apply the 80:20 rule (80% content marketing to 20% product marketing) until you know what works for your audience.

Using PLR for LinkedIn Discussion Groups (13)

A LinkedIn discussion is started by a member of a LinkedIn group who wants to gather opinions or answers on a particular topic.

Start off by joining Discussion Groups relevant to your field. Monitor these group discussions to find opportunities to add valuable counsel. By now, you have reviewed your PLR articles and they are ready to be used in a number of ways. This means that when you see a topic that you can contribute to, it will simply be a case of copying the most helpful section of your article, doing a quick review to make sure it's relevant to the discussion and then pasting your answer in the discussion feed.

Your reply to a LinkedIn discussion is limited to 2000 characters which is approximately 500 words. However, I recommend that you keep your message between 200 and 300 words. You can always include a link to the full information source if you need to.

The LinkedIn Help Centre provides the following advice when posting a link in a discussion:

"If you post a link into a discussion, you might see an error message that says "Please enter a valid URL". This sometimes happens if the link you posted goes directly to the main website page.

It's always best if your link goes directly to the article and not a main landing page. For example, it may not accept www.website.com, but it should accept www.website.com/article_name." (LinkedIn Help Centre)[viii]

LinkedIn discussions are more professional in nature than those posted on other social sharing networks. Keep your contribution relevant with the intention of helping the discussion owner find real answers.

LinkedIn is heavily monitored to minimize or remove any spam incidents. Focus on providing valuable information and members of the discussion that want to contact you will then send you a private message. The 80:20 rule does not apply to LinkedIn. LinkedIn should be 100% about the discussion and sharing.

Social Bookmarking and Social News sites

Social Bookmarking sites and Social News sites are often confused by web users since their features are so similar. Users often collectively referred to both of these as Social Bookmarking Sites. Having said this, there is enough difference to distinguish the two and this will influence how you use them to brand yourself.

Social Bookmarking Sites (14)

In essence, a social bookmarking site allows an internet user to bookmark a website that they've found interesting so that they can refer to it later. All these bookmarks are archived under your name on the social bookmarking site. It's similar to the bookmarking function in your browser except that it is stored online and you can share them with other people. By searching for a topic on these sites, a visitor is not only able to see which websites are related to the topic but also what other people thought of these sites.

The two most popular Social Bookmarking sites (in the true sense of bookmarking) are Del.icio.us (delicious.com) and StumbleUpon (stumbleupon.com).

How to use your PLR

As a business owner, you are able to become a member of these sites and then post interesting information that will point people to your business. The more information you post, the more traffic you'll be able to generate back to your business. There is also the benefit of creating backlinks when other visitors bookmark your information as interesting.

Each bookmarking site has their own set of rules about the amount of product marketing you're allowed to have in the articles or pages that you post. Be sure to read these and then adapt your customized PLR articles accordingly.

Social News Sites (15)

A Social News site also allows visitors to create indexes (or bookmarks) of interesting information. The difference is that the information on these sites is more dynamic, fast paced and newsworthy nature as opposed to the longevity of social bookmarking indexes. Social news sites therefore index items such as blogs, articles, news posts etc. Apart from indexing their favorite current events, visitors can also search and share news items and take part in discussions.

Popular social news sites are Digg (Digg.com) and Reddit (Reddit.com).

How to use your PLR

The more newsworthy your blog and website is, the more chance you'll have of being indexed on these news sites. Stay on top of the current affairs around your industry and be quick to comment on newsworthy events such as changes in regulation, crises in the industry etc. Blog immediately after news has broken by using relevant parts of your PLR to justify your opinions or show why you agree with the current event.

Engage In Online Forums (16)

An online forum is a discussion group where people from a common profession or people with a common goal "congregate" to get advice or to support each other. We looked at LinkedIn discussion groups earlier which can be consider a type of free forum.

Outside of LinkedIn, you'll find tons of forums on almost any topic. When you join a forum you will join many others from your profession as well as potential customers looking for answers from professionals.

Forum members are there to help each other by answering the questions of fellow forum members, or to get answers to their own questions. It is not a marketing and advertising site and overt marketing usually leads to guilty members being banned from the site unless the forum clearly allows self promotion. You will often find that members are allowed to market themselves openly on paid membership forums but not on free forums.

How to use your PLR

You can improve your reputation as an expert by being an active member of a forum - giving answers to as many questions as possible. Customized PLR can help you answer questions quickly and easily when the relevant topics are discussed. File your PLR in a well organized folder so that you can access and find information quickly. When you need it, simply copy and paste your answer into your forum response. Remember that you have already customized your PLR and the "copy-paste" is therefore not just a rehash of someone else's PLR.

Some forums allow you to add a link to your website into your signature. If your answers are helpful, you'll probably see some members click through to your website. Consider the forum rules before taking advantage of this marketing opportunity.

If sites don't allow you to refer to your business in the

signature, then be clear about who you are and where your business is based so that fellow forum members, who really want to track you down, can do so by searching for you on the internet. Don't use a pseudo name; you want people to know who you are.

Do an internet search for forums in your niche and join in on the discussions.

Media Sharing Sites (17)

This is the final category of our social media sites. Media Sharing Sites allow users to upload and share their photos, videos or audio files. The most popular sites are YouTube (www.youtube.com) for video and Flickr (www.flickr.com) for photo sharing. SoundCloud (www.soundcloud.com) is a popular option for sharing audio files.

How to use your PLR

It is relatively easy to create podcasts (audio files) and video from your PLR. We'll go into the detail later. Once these files have been created, sharing them is as easy as uploading them to the media sharing site and then letting your list know that they are there. Good indexing techniques will also help visitors find them in a Google Search.

Compile a schedule or plan (18)

By now you've already extracted a number of tips from your customized PLR. You can use the same tips on a plan or schedule for clients.

You can produce almost any generic plan for your customers to follow that will take them from a status quo to a desired state. Let's use the Success Coach as an example. You would be able to create plans like:

- 30 Days to Improved Health
- 10 Days to Better Concentration

- 30 Days to a More Confident You

Instead of writing this information as an article, you will compile a planner for the number of days in your heading.

Let's use an example of "30 Days to improved health". You can take tips from already customized health related PLR and slot them into a calendar format. Since you will need quite a few tips you will need to extract these from a series of customized articles. During the customization process, you would already have included your own tips from experience and you would have made 100% sure that you are satisfied with the information. Therefore this plan should be as simple as a "cut and paste" exercise, moving the tips from the PLR into a calendar format.

Use the tips, hints and facts from your PLR and rephrase them as action items. So if an original sentence reads:

> "Make sure you include enough vitamin C in your diet to control infection, neutralize free radicals and aid in the body's absorption of iron."

You will be specific about actionable steps in the plan. For example:

> "Day 2: Add 3 items to your shopping list that are rich in vitamin C. Include these in your daily intake throughout the week."

Use a calendar template and place an action item on each date. This is also a good way to point out any of your products that could assist your reader. But remember to keep the emphasis on the plan and not on your product recommendations.

Create a Checklist (19)

A checklist is another way to help your customer reach an end goal successfully. Its purpose is to help minimize mistakes or neglected steps in a process. It is not a list of full length step-by-step instructions explaining how each step can be achieved; it is simply the list of steps to be taken. Each item should be straightforward with a definite measure - you've either achieved it or you haven't. Unlike a calendar plan, you don't need to attach a specific date or timeline to the steps.

Once again, by branding the checklist, you not only show that you are an expert in the field but also that you care about the success of your customers.

You can easily create a checklist by combining the facts and tips you've extracted from your PLR. Rephrase each as an action item and list them in a particular sequence or group them in categories. Drop all unnecessary wording contained in the snippets and use only action points.

For example, our Freelance Accountant could release a "Checklist for gathering documents before tax return season":

Include a good introductory sentence from your PLR describing the need to be well prepared for your tax return.

Then introduce the checklist, and provide the actions.

1. Obtain the following documents from your employer:
   *   Document *a*
   *   document *b* etc.

2. Documents to get from your service providers:
   *   Document *c*
   *   document *d* etc.

3. Personal expense records:
   *   Document *e*
   *   document *f* etc.

4. Professional memberships and associations:
   *   Document *g*

- document *h* etc.

[Documents will vary depending on the country you're targeting].

Conclude the checklist by extracting a closing remark from a relevant PLR article.

Your customized PLR articles would have mentioned these categories and documents at various points. Simply extract these facts, and list them as actionable points under main categories.

The great thing about a checklist is that you can reuse it each tax season. You can also adapt it for customers in specific niches. For example:

- Tax documentation checklist for the full-time employee.
- Tax documentation checklist for the self-employed individual.
- Tax documentation checklist for the small business owner.
- Tax documentation for *any niche you support*.

There are many possibilities based on the audience you're trying to reach. Extract a good introductory sentence and closing statement from your PLR to round off the checklist.

Create a Worksheet (20)

Where a checklist is a list of definite steps that need to be taken, a worksheet is a set of factors to consider that will lead your customer through the high level steps but allows them to come to their own conclusions about the action points that need to be taken. This is a useful tool for your customers when there are no defined solutions to the choices that ought to be made.

The checklist example we used for the accountant contained very definite actions, not choices.

Let's use a new example of a small business owner - the owner of a catering service specializing in children's events.

To build your brand, you will provide useful information on all aspects of children's events and not just around the catering element. A worksheet with the aim of helping parents plan the perfect children's party is a great opportunity to do this.

The checklist could read something like this:
- Search for party venues in your area
- Inquire about availability on your party date
- Choose a party venue
- Book the party venue
- Agree the theme with the venue organizer etc.

A worksheet, on the other hand, allows more flexibility in the process by encouraging the reader to think through each point and come to their own conclusions. The simplest way to create a worksheet is to transform a checklist of action items into a worksheet format. Extract the "how to" or "step by step" instructions in appropriate PLR articles and rephrase each action item as a question. You can embed milestones in between the questions when a definite action step needs to be taken that doesn't require a lot of consideration, similar to our example of "book the venue".

Rephrase the action items as questions and provide space for the customer to fill in their own conclusions to each question. The worksheet could therefore read something like this:

What party venues exist in your area?

_____

_____

_____

Which are available on your preferred party date?

_____

_____

_____

Of these, which are your top three preferred choices and why?

Choose and book the venue.

What party themes have you and your child considered?

Which of these is the venue able to provide?

A worksheet can be considered a hands-off approach to coaching your customer through the process of making the decisions needed to reach their end goal.

In the process it also helps to brand you as an expert in the children's events niche. This impression of value-added expertise will draw clients to you even though you may never be involved in the actual venue selection for the party.

Your word processing software is more than sufficient to create a worksheet, which you can convert to PDF before placing it on your website ready for downloading. Include brief introductory and closing paragraphs to your worksheet component. Remember to brand the worksheet and include your contact details.

As with all our examples, you can choose to use a graphic designer to create a more professional look but it shouldn't be necessary.

Tip of the day/week/month (21)

Providing a regular tip is a technique that works well both online and offline. Dividing your information into quick, powerful pieces is just another way to exhibit your expertise.

How to use your PLR

You'll use your customized PLR in a similar way to the preparation of Facebook posts and Tweets. In fact you can use the same extracted facts - one sentence around 80 characters and no more than 120 characters. The only difference with the tips is the way you'll display the facts.

If you want to use the technique in your offline marketing then consider displaying your tips (one at a time) in or around your physical premises, or community areas where you might attract new customers.

Any business with a waiting or reception area has a captive audience. A medical professional can display facts or tips in their waiting area. Any business's reception can do the same. Think of any location where your customer will pause for long enough to read one sentence. Common examples include the entrance door to your offices, displays in your parking lot or on the inside of your lift. Remember to brand the message with your logo and contact details. An anonymous tip of the week in the lift will not do your brand any good.

You might want to hire a designer to create a template which you can use with each new tip. You'll only need to edit the text on your template and print it out each time you want to change the tip. More environmentally friendly methods include using an electronic notice board or a digital photo frame that can both display rotating tips.

You should also consider displaying your tips in messages that you already send to your customer. How about a one-liner on your statements?

If you have permission to market to customers' mobile phones you could send the tips to them via text message.

Create a "Top List" (22)

Audiences love lists, especially those that show the best of the best at one quick glance. They're informative and entertaining but they're easy to compile as a writer because you can include as much or as little detail as you want under each point. Some examples of "top lists" include":

- The top five reasons your child should play the piano.
- The top seven reasons you should hold on to your expense receipts.
- The top three wines of this season.
- The top ten reasons you should add honey to your shopping list.
- The top five ways to improve your concentration.

How to use your PLR

Your PLR is an easy way to whip up a list in no time. As with our previous examples, you can use the facts or tips extracted from your original PLR articles and combine them in interesting ways to make up the list. You can choose to give only a few words per bullet point or you can go into more details with each point.

You can use these lists very successfully in many of the online and offline media I refer to within the book.

11 COMBINING PLR ARTICLES

We've looked at some ways to use your PLR article by rewriting as well as repurposing it. We'll continue looking at repurposing the article by combining PLR articles, or parts thereof, to create longer pieces of information.

Create a special report (23)

A report differs from the other written forms of content we've looked at until now.

A report is a collection of factual content with the sole purpose of being a source of intelligence to the reader. It is not written in a conversational style and does not contain your opinions, personal views or personal experiences. It is raw data as it has been researched.

The objective is to allow the reader to come to their own conclusion about the topic. After reading your report, the reader decides if they want to pursue any of the resources and which sources of information they want to investigate further.

A report is usually between three and ten pages long and is written for a very specific part of your audience - the component that is looking for a more in depth knowledge of the subject.

How to use your PLR
You can easily create short reports by using the content of

several articles and combining them into a report format.

Review your customized PLR, extract the factual content and remove all mentions of your personal view or experience. Then add references to sources that you trust on the topic.

Here are some guidelines for your format:

1. Create a heading to tell readers what topic is being covered
2. Add a content page
3. Add a legal disclaimer since you cannot vouch for the accuracy of third party content
4. The introductory paragraph will explain which aspects of the topic will be covered
5. The body of the report is broken up into sections, each with a sub-heading of its own to help organize the information and for quick reference
6. Use the conclusion as an overview of the report
7. Always add a glossary of any technical terms or jargon
8. End off with a bibliography of resources you used (over and above your PLR) to help you write the report
9. Include your contact details
10. Add a title page or have a cover designed to give it a more professional feel
11. Add a header and footer section along with page numbering
12. Spruce up your report by making use of images and link to other related information.

Adding references to the body of your report

A report helps a reader make up their own mind about a topic, so keep it objective. Once you've inserted the facts from your articles, ask yourself the following questions and add the relevant information:

- Which websites can I refer my reader to?
- Which blogs can I refer my reader to?
- Are there any online forums that discuss this topic?
- Are there professional bodies that can be consulted?

- Are there products the reader could consider?

Simply create a section to list these resources each under its own sub-heading in the body of the report. When you are happy with your report save it as a PDF file and your report is ready to go.

Write a book (24)

This is perhaps a good time to pause and reflect on something that I hope has been clear throughout the book. Namely, the degree to which you should add your own voice to the PLR you purchase.

There are scores of PLR providers who claim that you can buy a pack of PLR articles or a PLR eBook, put your name on it and call yourself an expert.

While you are well within your rights to do so, this does not do justice to you as a legitimate expert. Am I saying you shouldn't be using PLR to write a book? Not at all. However, as with the majority of the techniques we've discussed, as an expert you need to respect your knowledge as well as your customer's right to hear your perspective on the topic. For this reason you need to customize your content, infuse it with your own style and add your personal points of view before using it as a message to your customers.

I would suggest that you apply this principle in a double dose when it comes to writing a book. Why do I feel this way? Because readers who buy your books do so believing that you are a credible, trustworthy source of information. This gives you a perfect opportunity to live up to that expectation by providing them with great views on the topic. If a reader likes your book, they are more likely buy your products or services.

How to use your PLR

I won't recommend that you take a pack of PLR and turn it into a book because you don't know how many other people have bought that same pack and created a similar book. Sales sites such as Amazon Kindle quickly pick up when books are too similar in nature and your book will be removed from their catalog.

My recommendation is that you use a unique combination of relevant articles from various PLR packs, or buy a unique combination of articles sold individually and use these as the basis of your chapters. This will help you create a unique book. In addition to the PLR articles, you need to incorporate your own personal learning and experience on the topic so that readers get the benefit of your insights.

In summary:

- Extract relevant articles from a variety of related PLR packs to use as the basis of your book.
- Don't use a PLR pack as is. In other words, don't buy a pack of ten articles and then create a ten chapter book from this. Chances are, someone else has already done this.
- The PLR content should form perhaps 40% - 60% of the final product; the rest should be a reflection of your own experiences, examples, case studies, opinions etc.
- Include facts from your own geography to make it unique to your local audience.

Yes, you can use PLR to help you generate your book, but out of respect for yourself and your reader, don't simply tweak a pack of PLR and call it your own. It becomes your own when you add your own flavor to the writing.

12 A CHANGE OF FORMAT

The techniques used up to this point have been changes to the written format of the PLR articles. We will now look at a few techniques that involve a complete change to the format of the articles.

PowerPoint slides (25)

One of the easiest ways to get more use out of your content is by turning simple articles into PowerPoint slides. It is very easy to dress up your articles by adding pictures, graphs and other illustrations. The design of your slides will also make the article appear completely different to the original plain text article.

The content of a PowerPoint presentation should mainly be key phrases and key words. You can use the presentation in a face to face format or as an online presentation. The intention is for the slides to keep a discussion on track but it is the presenter who should be providing the information.

How to use your PLR

Take a PLR article you want to discuss in a presentation. Use the highlights of the article as your main points. You can quote short sentences or definitions that explain key concepts if you need to, but in general, include a minimum number of sentences. A 400 word article will give you enough key points for about 10 to 12 slides which you can then use in various ways including offline workshops, presentations, business pitches or training interventions.

PowerPoint presentations can also be used online very successfully. There are media sharing sites set up to share slide presentations with the public. You can also automate the presentation, add background music and upload to a video sharing site like YouTube. One of the most exciting ways to use your slide deck is to create an MP4 video. This is done by using the slides as a foreground while you add a voiceover, music or any other type of audio to the background.

Brand each slide with your logo and include a link to your main business site.

Video scripting: from text to PowerPoint to video (26)

I mentioned before that your audience will have preferences in terms of how they choose to consume information. Video has become an increasingly popular way to spread information, because there is such a huge part of the global audience that prefers to consume their data via video.

To give you an idea of just how popular video messaging has become, YouTube alone receives over 1 billion unique visits each year, with over 6 billion hours of video watched each month and 100 hours of video uploaded every minute. (Social Stream Media)[ix]

These statistics for YouTube are astounding and yet YouTube is only one of the many popular online video sharing channels. It is certain that video is becoming one of the most popular information sharing formats on the internet.

Producing your own videos is easy for any business owner to do.

The easiest form of video is to use your branded PowerPoint slides, automate them and add a background music track. The better option is to use the same automated slides but to add a voiceover - yours or someone else's voice. The audience will hear your voice over the slides while viewing the images on the screen. These are great to start or update your YouTube presence.

Although this is a good start, you need to get to the point where you are comfortable having your face on video as opposed to only showing the PowerPoint slides. Adding the personal feel helps enable a sense of relationship, trust and loyalty with the viewer.

You can use your webcam, video camera or even a high quality mobile phone camera to record a video. If you are comfortable in front of the camera you could create a lot of content this way. If you find yourself talking for too long, then break the video up and you will have multiple days worth of content.

How to use your PLR

Each article you customize can become the content for a video. Use your customized article as a script. Adjust your voice to a more conversational but instructional style. If you want to create a series of useful video topics then buy a number of articles related to your business. Customize each one and turn each one into a video by either creating slides or by recording yourself talking through the content.

How to create a video

Creating a basic video is not that difficult at all. Most computers come with Windows Movie Maker and this is perfect for creating a video. If you don't have the program then you can download it, or any one of the many movie making programs available.

If you're using Windows Movie Maker then your first step is to create a PowerPoint presentation with your content, as described earlier. Just remember to add a slide that contains your URL so that people can visit your website. Then save your presentation as a JPEG file. Your next step is to open Windows Movie Maker and import your JPEG files. Drag each file down into your story board and add effects and a sound track or voice over.

There are many more video creation programs that do a similar job.

Once you are satisfied with your movie, save it as an MP4 and then upload it to any one of the free video sharing sites. Remember to share the video link with your network and also embed this video on your website.

Audio (27)

The general principle is that almost anything you can record on video, can also be recorded in audio. The exception would be in cases where your video is too heavily dependent on visual aids for the viewer to follow the message without them. An example is a step by step tutorial on how to install a WordPress blog. This would not be as effective on audio as it would be on video.

On the other hand, a video that is only uses PowerPoint slides to keep both viewer and presenter on track could just as easily be recorded on audio. Some people prefer to download audio information rather than video because audio has the added convenience of being more portable. Listeners can download and play audio in the car on the way to work, while waiting for the children at school or even while exercising.

The great thing is that, if you've created a video, you can easily convert it from MP4 (video) format to MP3 (audio) format without needing to re-record your message. It's quick, easy and could be free (depending on which resource you use).

Audio is also a great alternative for people who are not comfortable in front of the camera or who, for technical reasons, want to provide content as audio only.

There are great resources available for recording a podcast. Some of the free software provides the same quality as paid versions. Paid versions usually have more functionality and effects than free software. What makes a real difference is the quality of your microphone. There are many online tutorials about recording a podcast and our resource guide will also point you in the right direction.

How to use your PLR

Using PLR to record audio messages is similar to the way you would prepare a video message. The only difference is that you won't prepare visual aids in this instance - although you can use the PowerPoint presentation you've created as your cue cards.

Both with video and audio you need to write out your script and rehearse it until it comes across as a natural conversation. This will become easier with each new recording.

Include verbal references to your business during the podcast since the listener won't see the visual branding used in a video message. At the end of each podcast you can have a call to action to drive listeners to your website, product or service. If you do include a product promotion at the end then make sure that the podcast information is still useful should listeners decide not to purchase your product. At this point, your intention is to grow your brand. Give valuable content leaving your audience wanting more from your site or other product sales point.

Host a Webinar (28)

A webinar is an online conference where a host or presenter "meets" with an online audience using a computer and internet connection. Webinars work particularly well for live online training and information sharing.

Each participant sits in front of their own computer at home, in the office, or wherever they choose to be during the conference. As the presenter, you would host from your own computer. Your audience gets to see you or their slides - depending on which option you've chosen to use. You will not see the audience but can receive comments and questions from them.

The different types of webinar software offer a range of features. In general though, all the popular solutions are able to connect you, the host, to hundreds (sometimes thousands) of participants at one time. They also offer the option for a limited number of participants to phone in which is helpful for participants who don't have sufficient internet access to connect online. The popular software solutions also allows the host to record the webinar and then post the recording for those who could not attend live or who want to listen for a second time.

How to use your PLR

You can use your PLR to prepare for a webinar. Most of the work would have been done when preparing your PowerPoint slides, Audio or Video scripts.

If you choose the option of displaying visuals rather than speaking to the camera, then you could simply adapt your already customized PowerPoint slides to suit the audience you are targeting. Some hosts like to give their audience an opportunity to submit questions before the webinar date. By doing this you can prepare some slides to address specific questions in the event. If you don't have the questions beforehand, then allocate enough time to pause and address questions as they come in live. A good principle is to share your information for 3/4 of the allocated time and allow for questions and answers for 1/4 of the time. You can choose to address all questions at the end or as they come in - either way allocate enough time for the audience to take part. If you are hosting a particularly interactive and engaging topic then increase the question and answer allocation.

For your first few webinars, it is useful to have an assistant monitoring the questions and passing relevant ones on to you at the right time, rather than monitoring them yourself. You'll want to concentrate on using the technology and doing a great job presenting until you are confident enough to manage this on top of the comments panel.

If you are speaking to the camera rather than using slides, your PLR could be used to prepare a script. Since you're an expert in your field you will not need a word for word script but rather and outline of the points you want to make as well as the facts you don't want to forget. This is similar to the way you would have prepared for audio and video recordings. You can keep notes handy to glance at every now and then but don't read to your audience. Engage, and make "eye contact" with your camera as if you were in front of an audience.

Choosing a Webinar platform

My recommendation is to sign up for a number of free, live webinars - even if the topic is not in your exact field. Attend these live. This will give you a sense of how each platform works and which would suit your needs. Cost and customer recommendations are also key considerations. It's not necessary to invest a monthly contract fee if you're not going to host regular webinars. Start with one of the free options. You can upgrade or change providers if you choose to use webinars as a regular form of engagement - for free or paid advice.

Create an Infographic (29)

An infographic or "information graphic" is a visual display of information. It is a poster-like design which is easy to distribute, fun to read and contains a great deal of information.

Customer Magnetism is a Digital Marketing Agency based in Virginia, USA. I love the way they describe an infographic:

> "Infographics are a fun and quick way to learn about a topic without a ton of heavy reading. There are many different styles of infographics and data visualizations but the ultimate goal for all infographics is to be shared." (customer magnetism)[x]

The agency goes on to explain how high quality infographics are 30 times more likely to be read than text articles and that 40 % of our audience prefer visual information to text.

We've included an example in our resource pack for you to take a look at. Once you've seen what an infographic looks like, you'll begin to recognize them being used all over the internet and your social media connections.

An Infographic needs to be professionally designed and I recommend that you outsource this task unless you are a graphic designer. There are also companies that specialize in taking online orders for infographic designs.

How to use your PLR

Using PLR is simple. Use any of the combinations of PLR articles you've already prepared. Extract the facts you want to highlight to the reader. When you contact the designer, tell them about your audience, what you want to achieve with the infographic and where you plan to use it. Give them the information you want to get across and let them design it for you.

Once it's finalized, you can use the infographic on almost any of your offline or online media - provided it supports the use of graphics.

Online Pamphlet (30)

A downloadable pamphlet is a great way to combine images and text in a creative yet useful one-pager. Pamphlets are not as text heavy as newsletters or blogs but still contain more detail than a social media post can.

The Honey Farmer, for example, may want to create a series of pamphlets for readers to download. A honey related series may include topics like:
- Honey for enhanced health
- Recipes for the sweet tooth
- Unexpected uses for honey in the home etc.

A single page pamphlet is generally made up of three columns or panels, allowing you to put one sub-topic in each panel, for example, one recipe per panel with images that enhance the overall topic. Pamphlets look their best when there is a good balance of text, images and space. Don't overcrowd each panel. If your text is quite long, consider using a single, portrait page with only one recipe as opposed to three.

There are a number of ways to create your own pamphlets.

You can use PowerPoint to create your pamphlets. Choose the landscape orientation if you want to create panels or the portrait orientation if you don't want columns. Most word processing software comes with pre-loaded templates where you can choose the layout of your pamphlet and then simply populate it with text and images. Include the text you want from your PLR. Now add images.

For the more adventurous wanting to create a professional feel, there are a number of software packages that provide pre-designed templates where you literally only need to "drag-and-drop" your information.

Another alternative is, of course, to hire a graphic designer for the most professional designs and finishes.

How to use your PLR

You can use any of the articles that you have customized to create the pamphlets. Include the crux of the articles, for example the recipes, wound care instructions etc. Add a brief conversational-sounding introduction and closing to round the information off professionally.

13 GATEWAYS TO YOUR INFORMATION

The next section centers around using the products you've created with your PLR to attract more customers onto your list through different types of "gateways". Each gateway will help you grow your brand but without needing to make many or any further changes to your already customized PLR. You will simply need to choose which information you want to link the customer to via the gateway.

Create a Landing Page or Squeeze Page (31)

I touched on the concept of a squeeze pager earlier on in the book. As a reminder, it is an online form that captures a visitors email address and adds it to your marketing list with their permission. At the very least it requests an email address but you could also choose to collect other information to tell you more about the visitor. I find that the easiest way to create a squeeze page is to use the form creation tools provided by my autoresponder services.

Now you have a list of people that you can communicate with in future including marketing related messages. You can now begin to turn your visitors into customers.

Using your Information Products

A popular way to encourage website visitors to opt-in (or sign up) to your mailing list, is to give them something for free in return for their details. You can use almost any of the online products you've developed from your PLR the opt-in gift. How about your newly created eBook, report, slide sharing document or one of your videos? It doesn't have to be long but it does need to be relevant to your business and offer quality information.

Use QR (Quick Response) Codes (32)

A Quick Response or QR code is a square, bar-code looking image made up of a unique black and white stamped pattern on a solid color background. It's used quite widely in advertising.

You can think of it as being a hyperlink barcode. It's made to be scanned by a mobile phone when you take a photo of it using your phone's camera. This photo triggers an automatic reaction from the code which can either be that:

- the customer is connected to a business information site,
- the customer is sent information embedded in the coding of QR Code, or
- the customer's phone automatically performs a function chosen by the business. Amongst others, a customer's phone can be prompted to automatically:
  o send a tweet to your business Twitter account
  o dial your number
  o log onto your business Wi-Fi account
  o log onto your sales page with your special offer
  o make a Skype call to your business
  o access your Google map location
  o send a post to your Facebook page
  o connect to their PayPal payment page to buy one of your products

These are just a few of the possibilities of using a QR code.

There are many suppliers available who can create a QR code for you, some even providing this service for free. The site we've chosen is user-friendly, free and the QR code is ready to download in no time at all. We'll tell you more in our free resource report.

How to use your PLR

The information products you've created using PLR could be a huge benefit when you want to use PLR codes. Let's go back to our restaurant owner for a moment.

The restaurant can use a QR code to connect your customer to almost any of the information sources you've created from your PLR so far. Once you've decided what you want to prompt the customer to do you can:

- incorporate the code into the decor of the restaurant.
- display the code on each of your tables
- print it on your menu
- print it on your business card
- print it on the packaging of your after dinner mints
- print it directly onto your take away or leftover containers
- print it on stickers to paste on your takeaway or leftover containers
- print it on the next batch of customized serviettes you order.

Create a collection of QR codes, linking each to a specific action or information source. The QR code on the restaurant leftovers container could connect your customer to your blog where they can leave a comment about your service. The code on your menu could link them to more information about the nutritional value of each meal. As a restaurant owner, you will quickly identify opportunities to use your code.

This is a great way to connect an offline audience to your online content. People are curious and you'll find many people scanning the codes to see what they'll find on the other side of the gateway.

Regardless of the type of business you run, you can find ways to display the code. Print it anywhere your customer will be able to access it long enough to take a photo. This could be anywhere: business cards, brochures, t-shirts, any corporate wear, shop windows, office walls, posters, or any of the offline elements we've discussed in this book. You can even include it on your online platforms such as your LinkedIn and Facebook profiles.

Nowadays you can also create a QR code with a picture overlay in the shape of your logo or an image that represents your business. You can also customize the background color of the code. These two characteristics are particularly useful if you need customers to distinguish the difference in your collection of codes.

Using the codes will not only show that your business is in line with latest trends but will also provide a gateway to the information you want your customers to see..

14 YOUR NEXT STEPS

Feeling overwhelmed? Take it one step at a time

The options available to you may just leave you feeling overwhelmed. Even with the time and money that PLR will save you, how does a small business owner manage to market themselves using thirty or more techniques? The answer is to take it one step at a time.

Every story has a beginning. Yours is no exception. Your story has already started and marketing yourself is simply like putting pen to paper and fleshing out the story.

Where to start

Choose 2 or 3 techniques to implement. Master them. And then add more to your arsenal once the first few are part of your marketing routine.

My recommendation is to start by using your PLR to update your website and to add a blog. This gives you a point of reference - a home of information that you can refer people to.

Update your website with information that shows your expertise. Add pages such as:
- did you knows
- frequently asked questions about *the problem you're solving*
- the history of *your profession or product*
- free advice on *your field of expertise*

The discussions in your blog will show your visitors that you now only know what you're talking about but that you have your own opinion on the topic. You're open to sharing your thoughts AND more importantly to hearing and responding to the thoughts of others. The blog will make your site more dynamic, helping people find you through the search engines.

Once you've done this, begin to focus on the techniques that will reach the audience you need to attract the most urgently. Use offline techniques if you only want to focus on the audience in your vicinity or online techniques if you want to grow your list quickly from a broader reach.

Although you don't need to implement all 30 techniques, you most certainly can benefit from using as many as you can possibly work into your budget and schedule.

And now it's up to you

I trust that you've found this book useful. As you work with PLR you will find many more ways to use it simply because each business has unique content needs.

You may need PLR to supply information to noticed boards, information groups, business networking breakfasts or any other form of communication where you need to share information.

The key principle to keep in mind is simply this -

You can attract more customers to your business by sharing valuable information. We can help you save time and money in getting the information out there. How you package it depends entirely on how and where you want to grow your brand.

I wish you every success as you let your voice be heard.

Belinda

REFERENCES

[i] Joe Pulizzi. The History of Content Marketing [Infographic]. Content Marketing Institute. http://contentmarketinginstitute.com/2012/02/history-content-marketing-infographic/ (accessed February 13, 2014)

[ii] What is Content Marketing? Content Marketing Institute. http://contentmarketinginstitute.com/what-is-content-marketing/ (accessed February 7, 2014).

[iii] Google's Inside Search site. http://www.google.co.za/intl/en/insidesearch/howsearchworks/thestory/ (accessed February 14, 2014)

[iv] Royal Pingdom. Internet 2012 in Numbers. http://royal.pingdom.com/2013/01/16/internet-2012-in-numbers/ (accessed February 10, 2014)

[v] Heidi Cohen. 20 Experts Weigh in on Repurposing Content Marketing. http://heidicohen.com/how-to-reuse-your-content-marketing/ (accessed 10 February, 2014)

[vi] eBiz MBA. Top 15 Most Popular Social Networking Sites. http://www.ebizmba.com/articles/social-networking-websites / (accessed February 13, 2014)

[vii] Beth Belle Cooper. 10 Surprising New Twitter Stats to Help You Reach More Followers. http://blog.bufferapp.com/10-new-twitter-stats-twitter-statistics-to-help-you-reach-your-followers (accessed February 14, 2014)

[viii] LinkedIn Help Centre. Post Length in Group Discussions. http://community.linkedin.com/questions/5066/post-length-in-group-discussions.html (accessed 17 February, 2014)

[ix] Social Stream Media. http://www.slideshare.net/SocialStrand/social-media-stats-2014 (accessed 10 February, 2014)

[x] Customer Magnetism. What is an Infographic? http://www.customermagnetism.com/infographics/what-is-an-infographic/ (accessed 17 February, 2014)

Remember to download your free book bonuses and more at

www.thecommunicationshop.com

under the tab "Say More by Doing Less"

www.ingramcontent.com/pod-product-compliance
Lightning Source LLC
Chambersburg PA
CBHW060623210326
41520CB00010B/1455